Wombats

My First Picture Book

Steve Parish
PUBLISHING
www.steveparish.com.au

Wombats belong to a group of animals called mammals.

Common wombat

Mammals that have a pouch for their babies are called marsupials.

Common wombat and young

A wombat digs a burrow in soft earth.
The burrow keeps it safe and warm.

Southern hairy-nosed wombat

Wombats will hide in a hollow log if they are in danger.

Common wombat

Wombats live mostly by themselves.

Common wombat

Wombats usually sleep all day.
They are nocturnal.

Common wombat

A wombat comes out at night to find food. It eats grass and other plants.

Common wombat

A wombat may have to walk a long way to find food.

Common wombat

A wombat has strong legs for walking.

Common wombat

A wombat has sharp claws for digging.

Common wombat

A female wombat has a pouch that faces backwards. This keeps the dirt out.

Common wombat

A baby will stay in the pouch until it is strong enough to walk with its mother.

Common wombat and young

Most wombats have grey fur but some have brown or black fur.

Common wombat

This southern hairy-nosed wombat has grey fur that is soft and silky.

Southern hairy-nosed wombat

A wombat

is protected by thick soft fur that may be grey, brown or black.
Southern hairy-nosed wombat
has small ears. Common wombats have small, rounded ears. Hairy-nosed wombats (like this one) have larger, more pointed ears.
has small eyes.
has a pouch that faces backwards.
has a large, bare nose. Hairy-nosed wombats have a hairy muzzle, but common wombats do not.
has sharp claws for digging.